Wolf and Amaryllis:

A Collection of Poetry

by

Sebastian Guyette

DORRANCE
PUBLISHING CO
EST. 1920
PITTSBURGH, PENNSYLVANIA 15238

Dorrance Publishing Co
585 Alpha Drive
Suite 103
Pittsburgh, PA 15238
Visit our website at *www.dorrancebookstore.com*

ISBN: 979-8-8868-3067-5
eISBN: 979-8-8868-3927-2

Contents

The Line

Life is filled with feelings and emotions
With force and how much exertion
It's filled with pain and hurting
It's filled with other people flirting
There are stories and people who everyone knows
And there are ones that are hidden away
People that attention to is no longer a must to pay
A path of many takings
Bodies filled with whispers and aching
Milestones and stoning miles
Different people, different styles
Lines that divide in physical sense and mentality
No more can you feel the world for what it was
It was changed
The world is defined
It's defined by the person and the holding of their mind
So the world to your mind is confined and defined
A void is left in my mind and now my world
For my definition of the world and my life is different now
There's a line
Before and after, that is all I know for tragedy
Mine filled with agony caused by absence
Of a thing or person I had once
An imperfect imbalance
A tragedy and mask on me
What was once forgotten and now remembered...gravity
Reality

No amorality
No more euphoria
Gravity exists and so does where it leads
My world is changed
Now it's boring and arranged
Organized and strange
Unlike what I wanted
Different from what it was
Halted and haunted

The Faded Idea of Love

I can't handle this agony and absence
My mind is speaking in fragments
My heart is confused and erratic
And my brain feels like an attic
It is cluttered, it is sporadic

I guess in a way it is connected
But my actions don't reflect it
My mind is speaking in fragments with my brain that's like an attic
In a way that makes me seem like an addict

I'm addicted to love
I'm addicted to the feelings it can create
When you truly feel something for someone,
No one, not even you can ever relate
Those moments are felt intensely,
And you feel in those moments,
Immensely

Such powerful love can only end in disappointment
It will flatline and cause you pain
That pain may vary
Depending on the depth of love that you may carry
But this pain is something that kills you
You may not die from it
(But you very well could)
But it kills you

It destroys this idea of this love you thought existed

Your heart will be dormant and empty
It wants to be alive, but it can't be
It was fed ideas that can't be
It desires to be those ideas, but it just can't be
It's just not that simple and no one will be able to see

I wonder if anyone besides the person in your head ever notices
That you are not the same person
That your old person is dead
It's as if the ego was killed, faded, and won't build
It's freezing over, and sometimes it feels like it might uncover
But then you're reminded that it's just too wounded to heal
That you're just not able to feel

Nothing can break the seal,
Its hold is too strong
It's like a scar in your soul,
It may be able to put itself back together,
But it will never be together like it was at the point before,
It will look different despite how hard the body tries to heal,
It is constant and you are reminded of it frequently,
It's always there and is a part of you

I wish I could start over; I wish I could start new
I wish I could experience more and enjoy life a little more
I want to forget; I want to be able to close that door
But the cold gust from the sealed heart keeps blowing it open

I used to be creative, but now I'm getting dull
My heart is fed up with ice, and it's grumbling, but it's full

The idea of love is such a faded one
It's no longer a thought,
You already thought you had it once,
That it was over and done, and true love was caught

The idea of love was infinite, but now it is a faded one
I can't feel anymore
And I want to feel again

Valentine

Will you be my Valentine?
I've liked you for quite some time
Will you be my Valentine?
If even the sun didn't rise...
And the sun didn't shine
All I want is for you to be mine
If there was no light and only darkness
I still would want you to be mine with whole heartedness
Regardless, if your answer is yes or no
It doesn't stop me from wanting to know
This feeling I have fills me from head to toe
There is just something I'm just dying to know
And that is
Will you be my Valentine?
Just this one time?

The Music, The Orchid, The Vampire

I can't design myself to love you any less
You are the music in my heart
And I never want us to drift apart
I'm designed to listen to you
I'm programmed to do whatever it takes to be with you
I'm uncontrollably always trying for your attention
The musical waves flutter in my chest
The musical waves project from my chest
My heart is a crest for love that never becomes less

The waves pound in my heart
They're what keep it beating
They're what keep it consistent
Your heart needs consistency
If you don't want to die from inefficiency
You give me those waves
You give me that consistency
To my heart and brain, you are beautiful mystery
Systematically and dramatically
I can't give you up
You are what gives me life
You are what makes the word "life" have meaning

With you, the before darkness line of my future
That dark line now has a gleaning
A gleaning of light
A future that's more realistically in sight

You can make me weak
But you also give me might
With you, I want nothing more than to fight
To fight for that gleaning light in my future
No matter how small
I'll die for that light
I'll die for that chance

Like an orchid
She is an angel
Like an orchid
She is vampire
She is an angel for her display
And a vampire for her stagnant compelling attraction
Stagnant because she can sit and do nothing
And I will always want to do something
I will always feel something
She's a vampire for her temptation
A vampire for the sensation

My heart thrives for that sensation
The feeling of my lips on the tips of hers
That's enough to drive me crazy
That's enough to drive me to insanity
That feeling allows me to thrive for humanity
Because with humanity comes pureness
And lasting dreams of the simplest things

Those simple things are more like stepping stones to more
They are little things on the floor
Things you may not pay attention to
Like sand on the shore

Those simple things are part of what makes us whole
Without one grain of sand
A beach is still a beach
But without sand
There is no beach
Simple things like your glare or your stare
Keep me on edge
On edge of my stair
Waiting to see if there's another step in the story
Another step to more flare
Of more caring of something more we might share

I want to share something with you
I want to share a flare
I want to share our care
Care for each other
Only you
Only us
No care for any other

Restlessness

I'm wide awake
And I can't sleep
The only thing on my mind
Just makes me weep
It's ten at night
And my chest is tight
My feelings just aren't right
There's nothing I can do
I can't fight
I can't go to bed but that would be my highlight
I just lost my highlight
My light that shone ever so bright
Yet I lost it
I lost it and it's out of sight
There's nothing I can do to retrieve that light
Nothing about this night brings me any delight
I need something to act as a satellite
No person can do that for me
That's why I write
I'm bawling my eyes out
I'm stalling because of doubt
I want to scream
And I want to shout
But I can't because of the people about
So I sit, sigh, and cry in silence
I just want to punch the wall
But I can't result in violence

I have school tomorrow

And I won't be able to sleep

Is it possible to feel any more hollow?

My battery is slowly draining

But I have to be more constraining

And do the best with what's remaining

But my bones can't stop aching and straining

Let's stop blaming because that's not entertaining

But my hope is waning

My arms are weak and shaking

My whole body is quaking

I want to be loud and let it out

But I can't because I don't want anybody waking

I guess life is just one big painting

You are the artist

The world is your canvas

But sometimes when things don't go your way

You have to improvise

And when you improvise

Your original idea, to your surprise

Was not as good as when you improvised

So I exercise knowing I lost the biggest prize

And when I do that it takes my mind of her beautiful eyes

And other feelings besides the emotional pain begin to rise

I just need to take my mind off the butterflies

I need to do whatever it takes to make my mind randomize

Instead of categorize

All the feelings she gave me inside

I never felt so alive

But it's over now

I just have to survive tonight and try not to recite the past

But I know I will anyways because the feelings were real

With her everything was electrified and maximized
Not a single thing was televised
She was my paradise
She left me mesmerized
But I rolled the dice
And I lost
And all I do is want to apologize
But she left me
So I have to get rid of the envy
So I don't end up crying next time she sits next to me
But all these feelings are heavy
And being her best friend
I'm not ready
I hope she can understand
Because being close to her already
That will be deadly to me
So I just have to take my mind off of it gently
And call it a night
But I can't sleep
So I'll have to call it a write

Waterfall

There seems to be this waterfall that flows upon the surface
It starts from the top and reaches its lengths to the lowest points
It seems to thrive to find even lower points
Every person contains a world
In every person there is a waterfall
The waterfall only flows when a new point can be reached
Some get tougher and it gets harder to find any place lower
Yet one always arrives.
There seems to be a tree that stands strong at the center of every forest
This tree has lasted so long, but its strength will get weaker
This process can and easily will be sped up
It can be tarnished and broken, but as long as it stands, so does the forest
It's the elder to the being of the trees that it surrounds
As long as it exists, so does the forest,
However, if it may fall, every other part of the forest soon will follow
They all rely on this one tree to keep the forest united and flowing

There seem to be this sky, above everything, and it keeps the trees alive
This sky allows water to be given and water to be taken
The sky may be very powerful, but it is quite fragile
It is often attacked more, the longer it exists
There is no escape from every instance that occurs
And every instance that occurs has its own impact.

Tears, the heart, and the mind

Without View

You...
You make me laugh
You make me smile
You make me think everything was worth while
A moment with you is a moment that is true
In every light, in every darkness
With you, there is still a beautiful hue
I wish for a lifetime of laughs and smiles and beautiful, time-filled miles
A lifetime without you is a lifetime without hue, without truth,
and without view
Without view is without a good horizon
Without view is without the sight, the memory of us
The sight that fills me with endless joy
A sight that I wish to be with forever, and a feeling that can never sever
Without view is without you
And without you is a moment of desire
I desire the sight, the might, the flight, and the light
The sight of your smile and the might that you give me where I
can walk endless miles
You give me the feeling that I am flying, soaring above all problems
Soaring next to the solution, absolutely no delusion or dilution
The light is a light telling me we're meant to be
Seemingly from the heavens, you're a blessing that beckons
Your presence is overwhelming, and it feels as if my hold on the
earth lessens
It feels as if I've grown wings and gravity no longer applies
This feeling, it isn't demise, but this feeling it makes me rise

As if close to the stars, close to the skies, close to the beauty of af-
terlife that lies
Lies there in my heart when you're around
This feeling
It's ecstatically profound
Every second, every day, every passing minute that lay
I realize I want to be with you
And with you, I want to stay
I never had much faith, but for that I pray
Just another day with you
I wish for that and another kiss, too
I don't know what you're gonna feel about what I have said and
what I'm gonna say
But baby, I'm missing you
I've never said anything more true

Yellow Flower

Vulnerable but strong, heartbroken, yet bold,
open yourself to me and unfold,
your beauty lies beyond just your image,
deep inside is maybe the greatest beauty you hold,

Laugh of the dandelions, you soak the sun, and glow with its rays,
so much on your mind,
counting your days,
everything you do,
it's insane the effort and quality you bring, deserving endless praise

I love the encounter of you and your embrace
The air around you moves in insane ways that just make my heart
and mind levitate with an air of their own hoping to blend with yours,
unity, pureness, and a person I adore,
you're a dandelion on a beach where none other dare to venture,
but you're the bold,
you're the determined and a great future foretold,

Looking into eyes like yours that hold light so intense,
the way you make that light bend with the gravity of the depth
that yourself can't comprehend
without the spirit of being the observer,
with whites that rival even smooth fresh opened paper,
yet not as flimsy, far more bold,
Dandelion, enjoy yourself, enjoy your depth, and all the gravity
you hold

As a Teenager, with a Teenager

I'm a teenager

Finding real love is really rare

I've given up

I don't care

I've done my best

It just left me in a mess

I've lost my hope

I thought with enough hope and dedication,

Even if without relaxation

You can achieve anything

I lost that ideal

I lost the appeal

Friends are what keep you strong

They are the ones that belong and always stay

True friends will never fly away

They'll stay and be there in the darkest times

And bring you to the brightest height

Like love, they can give you the greatest might, it just lasts longer

True love is a drug and makes you feel amazing

But like every drug, there's usually a downfall

And love's downfall is excruciating and painful

And even so, I still can say the feeling of love can still outweigh

Why look for love if it fails anyway?

I'm done trying

I'm done looking

I'm a teenager

There's no point

I believe in love that lasts forever

But I don't believe I'll find that with a teenager

All There Is, Is You

Already I can feel my feelings for you grow
Looking at you makes me think how much you mean to me, I can
Look at you and constantly get my mind sweeped

The thought of you makes me weak
Hearing your voice makes me weak
Endlessly playing our days alone makes me weak
Reluctantly I can see me and you can possibly be meant to be
Except there are obvious obstacles
In life you are filled with choices and decisions
So many choices and decisions...
In my mind I do know that I am willing to go the distance
So, I will go and I will know that you in my life gives me new existence
You change the meaning of love for me
Or do you just add more to it?
Unfortunately, I can't really answer
But I can say
Love is a wide variety of things
And you hit more off that variety than I ever felt before
The feelings I have for you I can't help but adore
And being with you makes me always want more
The time I spent with you
The time I do spend with you
The time I got to share with you

The time I do share with you
All of that time is seamless

My feelings for you only grow
They grow to the point where I don't know how much of it to show
Sometimes I get confused if I should show less or more finesse
More or less I do show more and with finesse
And when I think of you, everything else becomes less and less
And my mind just becomes a mess
To the point where I need to rest to get my mind off of you
But all there is, is you
When you say you're "eww"
I can't help but think how that's not even close to true
Because thinking of you and you're eyes and their perfect shade of
blue
All that leads up to is me thinking how unbelievably not true
You can try to argue but
I love you
And that IS true
All there is
Is you

Bell

Golden border, with just a crack...
I want to hear your sound,
I want to get it back,
Let me hear your voice once more...
It has a special ring...
With that special ring, only beauties can you sing.

You sing to my heart, and I can feel it deep inside me,
Everything has a uniqueness,
And yours is what drives me,
You have an inner pendulum,
It likes to swing one way,
Before at last it reaches a certain point and will no longer stay,
It will linger for a bit, and then it will go out with coalescence,
It produces something auditory of an angel, a sweet simple essence,
The spell does break, so then it can repeat,
The pendulum will swing back the other way,
But never takes a seat,
My feelings for you grow day by day,
As I get to hear you sing my nights away...
Sweet, simple bell...
You gave me heaven, but now I'm handed hell

Continuity of the Triangle

Feelings exert
Feelings expose
There are many things in this world
Many things that have been chose
Feelings exploit
Feelings impose
Many things came to sight
All things rose

A tale of two lovers entwined with another
One feels a shutter
and soaring winds flutter
Breezes blow of uniting and gusts filled with fighting
For a small time
It felt exciting

It started gathered in a basement
We were celebrating
For a second, she felt something
That later she felt as a mistake
A misplacement
They were dating
But this day after, she was absent him
And he was a perfect replacement
He was a substitute
But this day on blossomed days filled with joy
They were resolute

She liked him and he liked her, too
He knew the outcome
But thought he could fight it back
The days where he loved her
That love everyday would recur but stronger
I was confused
This was madness!
Days were filled with sadness, madness, love, and restrain
All of which things packed together can cause great pain
But I like it anyway because of the love that sang
The love was great and it was feign
I had to hide it and put it to the side then
She didn't want me to tell anyone
No one to confide in

She seemed like a flower from the greatest garden
Eventually they'd have to pardon
Because him in her life didn't make sense
And he thought to himself
This going his way was unlikely
His heart and mind were very tense
He was on the fence
There was a battle between his logical mind and loving heart
She was immaculate
The battle was intense
She was amazing
She had an effect that made his mind dense
He thrived on his heart
And she filled it
To him, she had a heart of gold
That he wanted to be a part of
He had a dream with her

They were together
He wanted to fulfill that dream
By whatever means

Now
The girl was deciding but couldn't make a choice
Isabella, she was fighting but couldn't rejoice
The situation was a burden
She didn't want to hurt him
Jake wanted her happiness
But that he couldn't give to her

Her feelings for Joseph were still strong
Jake knew this but hoped he was wrong
Her decision took a while, and it took too long
The story started to sweeten like a beautiful song
She told Joe always
Now it was never
Jake was a burden and that promise she couldn't sever
He saw this and pushed her astray
He told her that this is the only way
She accepted without hesitation
He just hoped he'd stay in her heart
To him, it was the greatest destination

They fell apart but stood by a string
He felt his choice was right
But was robbed of any might
He had a feeling in his chest
A feeling that stings
And pulled at his heartstrings
He heard a whisper that rings

A whisper carrying many things
Those things, throughout his body, sing
With bad situation it brings

This all started on a whim
She was in love with Joe
But couldn't deny what she felt for Jake
She still had feelings for him
Yet his chances were very slim
They still had a connection
She still had affection
He couldn't control himself
Jake tried to do the right thing
But that whisper from his heart
Was pulling him apart
Something of sadness and pain will start

Isabella met Jake for secret hugs and kisses
Which brought upon his wishes
For even more with the Missus
But the pain was vicious and could never be cured
She was alluring
His love for her was deep, it was secured
She was with another, but he endured

Many occurring instances
Many distances
Many witnesses

They showed their love endlessly
And it hurt
He was an outsider to their life

And just brought much strife
The two lovers, Isabella and Joe
Fought constantly
Jack was always shocked to see...
His poetry was his therapy

In the middle is where he lies
Desperate for her love
It hurts
Half the time he sees her is with another guy
Every time passing by
His eyes fill up, and he wants to cry
To see her with someone else
Just mortified
Cast with sighs
And endless red eyes

Whenever they were together
His mind got stormy
Everything turned to bad weather
She swore to him and it made it all better
He wished that he took the opportunity when he first met her
Now he's mixed up in the center

They still exchanged messages of lovers
Jack's heart belonged to one
Isabella's to two
She was his sun
He was her taboo
They hung out and acted as a single
It was sinful
But it felt like love

To him, a perfect fit
If only she put him above

He couldn't control himself
Jack couldn't get enough
She was beautiful
His weakness
Doing the right thing, it was rough

It started to get harder
The pain strengthened
He just wanted to have a start with her
Jake couldn't stand it
He was again reaching a limit
His heart was shattered
She really mattered
His heart was broken and corrupt
It was love at its darkest degree
But the love was greater than the eye
Greater than you can see
Above even the sky
Wider than any ocean or sea
But it was filled with debris
And that was easy to see
This love, it came with a fee

A few weeks passed by with the same thing
Painful pulling at the heart
She was being torn apart
With Jack, she wanted a start
But she didn't want an end
She was trying to defend

Isabelle didn't want to be hurt
She didn't want him to be a flirt
Jake would hurt her
He doesn't understand
Can't let him in
He'll fade
He won't love me
It's just a charade
With Joe, a possible future can be made
With Jake, for her, it was uncertain
Who is he?
What kind of person?
Isabelle was hiding behind a curtain
I'll hurt him...

I don't see what he sees in me
He'll get to know, then he'll flee from me
He'll get the key and won't like what he sees
He'll unlock me and leave to be free from me
I guarantee
He'll like me just for the sensuality
He won't be able to handle
The flame will go away
This relationship is just a candle
A scandal, it will dismantle
It's too much of a gamble

Difficult Times

My pants are stained

I'm walking in the rain

My feelings can't be restrained

Sadness and love reign

Thoughts are overwhelming

My spirit feels like it's almost swelling

I can hear the pitter patter and the sound of the rain in the well ring

Usually, you can hear animals here but because of the weather

They won't sing

The old man sitting on the porch near me has just spoken

Please be quiet

I don't want my young ones to be awoken

So I tried to be silent

I tried to be silent in this small world of strident

In my own mind

My own thoughts

I confided

On this very street, a criminal was sighted

I could see the sirens

I can see two men fighting

One of the men was well known

He was considered criminally insane

But was still able to buy guns

Then a guy came and tried to bend my thumbs

A guy was shot

Multiple bullets

A single was all it took

But he shot more

And of all his few bullets

He wasted nine ones

The intensity level heightens

Another one comes up to me

He runs

A guy told me to get out of here

This entire situation made me out to be a deer

I felt hunted

While I was running

I tripped

My speed was stunted

"Run, unless you want to see red!"

I regained my balance and I sped

All of this is from a memory in my head from when I was eight

My younger life wasn't that great

In the streets, I always felt like bait

My thoughts were mine

In which I carried and conveyed

I felt disdain

I was still in the rain

No one came

I never looked at life the same

I snuck back in when I heard the train

What was said next was feigned

I'm sober, I promise

I PROMISE ON MY DEAD UNCLE CHARLES

My dead great uncle's name was Thomas

So much for that promise

She was a novice at honesty

And modest when it came to drinking tonic flawlessly

She was lawless

She was lost

All the cigarettes

All the alcohol

She didn't know the cost

She didn't know the toll

Until all of what was important was sold

If she only kept true to a promise that she ended up locking in a closet

Maybe in my life she could be there

Maybe in my life she could be less rare

Just one promise!

Does that not seem fair?

Why couldn't she just care?

It's not like her to care?

She wouldn't dare

Especially when she drinks

If she didn't drink, this wouldn't occur

She wasn't sober

And all I wanted

Was just one last promise

That didn't end in a blur

One last moment with her

Instead I ended up with a cop as my chauffeur

In the back of the car crying

Thinking of her

I ended up sighing
It's her choice
She's just quickly dying
And as time goes on
My memories with her are frying
All because she was lying

Darkness Vs. Light

The darkness inside fills our outer demise in the skies
and when the darkness inside fills our soul and gives us a toll, we
need to open our eyes
People around, sounds are profound but the real issue,
Now, the real issue is a lack of knowledge of what we do.

The light starts to hide away, and the soul keeps screaming, "Get away!"
It's tempered and it has something to say,
It's so confused and conceived in darkness that it now pushes
those that can make it go,
but it just goes astray
The darkness just unfolds and picks its spot and there it will lay
And day by day can pass,
And you're busting your ass
Time is moving fast
and life can quickly pass.

Confinement is a toll that keeps our heaven on hold
We take the light, we toss it away for the darkness that is more bold
When light tries entering our life,
To try to warn us of the darkness,
The consumption doesn't like what it's told
As time passes and passes, we get more old
But what old is, keeps shrinking and shrinking.

Darkness vs Light, it really gets you thinking...

Do You Ever Know Love?

How do you ever know for sure if you've experienced love?
Time passes and you meet someone else
They can be similar or different in every way
You could have known them for a smaller period and have grown
more fond
Your definition changes
Your traditions change
Birthdays, anniversaries, rearranged
Past experiences estranged
Tossed up in a timely angle, turning, tangle
You swear you know love
You swear you've experienced it at its greatest degree
But you eventually slip out of that relationship with ease
Moving on to the next person to please
Your heart races
You're astounded
Heart throbbing, blood pumping, feelings in your head pounded
New feelings, they weren't around then
Things tingle, nerves extend to every end, broken feelings can
never mend
Masking the pain lasting
Set in a cycle of bet
Ex key holders
New people you have met
Opening the door and finding the key to your heart
Shaved and ripped apart
Stitched together with simple compliments

Not enough string so the heart is tense
The next one is greater than before
With her, you simply want more
Love from the others?
Was it love?
What I feel with this person
It doesn't compare
Everything. every moment we share
Now more than ever, I really care
But I swore I knew love
I swore that was its peak
It was hopeless for anything more to seek
But records of feelings and depth were broken
So do you ever know love?
It changes all the time
It's modified by the millennial mind
Don't submit to love you see
Take a deep breath, just breathe
The love is already defined
Love is known and forgotten
Don't be a victim to a fake
Because those feelings?
They don't shake
One day you'll make it
You'll find the people and person you need
Then you'll be freed
It is a seed
It takes a while to grow to its highest point
Be patient
This is your life, take time, don't waste it

Dream of a Bear

Who am I?
What a cliché poem starter
But the question remains
And finding the answer keeps getting harder and harder
Every day I wake up and look into the mirror
I get lost in thought
Thinking about my day
Today and the days before
But what for?
What am I trying to achieve?
What is it that I aim for?
Then I realized I don't really have any goals
And there's nothing really that I want more
My life is really just a bore
But why is it that I don't want more?
You'd think someone like me would want something else
But I don't really think about anything else
What I have now is what I have now
There's nothing else to make of it
So why throw a fit?
Part of me just doesn't care
Should I?
What if I become someone or something that I wouldn't be able to bare
I had a dream
And in that dream, I was being chased by a bear
There was a big black figure in the meek, shallow woods
This shadow blended in so well with its background

That's because of its hair
And its hair was dark brown
Much like my own
Might I share something with this bear?
This bear...
It may start to get aggressive
But in this moment that I shared with this bear
This small moment of despair
We looked into each other's eyes
What beautiful, big luxurious eyes
I got her by surprise
I could see the scared look in her eyes
But even though she was scared
She thought I was a threat and hid her cubs and put herself out in guise
This bear only acted out of its despair and its fear
It's fear, for her babies were here
She didn't want them to be hurt
So she was putting herself out to be hurt
Out there willing to hurt
How selfless of a bear
In a few moments
I might just be selfless because of the bear
But in the moment that I share
I didn't care
But now I'm on my feet running
Running from the bear that is way more cunning
This mom, she had something to fight for
She had a purpose
A purpose she would gladly die for
Deep down she was scared
She glared
Didn't even frown

But deep down
I can see it in her eyes
Deep down
She was willing to cry
But no matter how much she wanted to
She didn't let herself because she was trying to be strong
But this strong mom, she lost anyways
She ended up being surrounded by a pack of wolves
That saved my life
But I can't say the same for one of her cubs
One of them died from the wolves
And the mother cried for her lost one
She was surrounded and wanted to escape
But there weren't any ways she could have evaded
So she wailed and she cried
She let all her pain out
The wolves were just about done with her
She was so emotionally and physically hurt now
She coughed and out came a gush of blood
She looked as if she was ready to give up
But she didn't give up
She fought back even when she was so outnumbered
But she fought back because her children were numbered
She lost one
That gave her more reason than ever to get clever
So she did, and she spited all of the wolves
And left them eradicated
So I took the chance she couldn't
And I evaded
But as happy as I was to get away
I was happy that the bear also got away
Keep in mind, this is the same bear that was ready to kill me out

of shallow-aimed despair
What can I say?
This bear triumphed today
I want my life to have meaning like that
Hopefully minus the combat
But that combat was symbolic
I don't have well-defined goals
I just know
I don't want to be another alcoholic

Entropy vs. Nature

Our life is kind of cruel if you ask me
The entire existence of us coming to be?
There's two forces working at us
They're internal and external
The history of this battle foresees us
and hardly is at a cusp
It pulls you apart, it fragments you
One force atomizes you and sees you for what you truly are
But what you truly are, is that truly you?
Our bodies are so intricately constructed
So beautifully represented
Nature has allowed us to be
How do people define Nature?
What shall become of it?
Is our definition perhaps off some?
Say it's unity
Say it's oneness
The plants, animals, and even the protists
Beyond that...the atoms, the planets, the galaxy, the universe, the
cosmos
Oneness and order
It just seems to be
Yet even so, even in the order,
Things are so random, so out of place
Just take the human race
In Physics, one might learn that for every action,
There is an equal and opposite reaction.

Extrapolate this some, and realize
For life there must be death
For expansion there must be dis-expansion
Now that doesn't quite make sense.
There is something unfathomable outside our spectrum of thought
For there to be a beginning, there must be an end
For there to exist something, there must be a boundary
What lays out of a boundary?
The cosmos expand and contract
We are the sweet spot that every other place lacks
Perhaps two types of nothing do in fact make something?
Despite what everyone can comprehend
Nothing is never really nothing
If one thing was united, for example, a canvas of black
If that's all there is, just black, and nothing else,
if that's all you ever knew, is it nothing?
If there is some space out in existence with chaotic static,
and that's all you ever knew, is it nothing?

Gone Anyway

How long does it take?
Before the feelings finally shake?
Before the pain and loss are gone
Simple things pondered upon
Hours spent wasted away
Thinking of things that are gone anyway

Hope for Fate

Dance with me
Twirl me around like a memory with a beautiful melody
You're meant for me
Taking on the world and our issues
We're bold
My soul was sold
It turned to coal
Hysterically, it's cold
The heart remains gold

Wishing up things like a weak mind on Hennessy
Remembering, we're meant to be
—Some things that are meant to be, shatter up and the remains
are empty

Crescent
Sweet, simple, surplus, luminescent
Stars -bright that shines on a plaster of dark
(oo let's wish on that one)

Time engulfed furiosity
Simple pleasures, lost with glee
Sharing a moment under the sky
(let's call that one ours)
Stars holding memory for future descent with feelings that are left
at sea
I swear... we're meant to be

Ivory

Ryleigh, you're like piano keys
Not a fake piano, not a keyboard
You're a real expensive, genuine piano
You're a specialty, you're a fine wine
You would be the center of events at any expensive or less, fancy dine
You have a fragrance sweeter than the potency of trees and pine in
a pinewood forest
You have depths deeper than the ocean in your eyes
Don't mistake that I'm comparing her eyes to the ocean
No, I'm comparing the ocean to hers
Because her eyes are of greater beauty, so that's the standard that's set
A standard the ocean has not quite yet met
Ryleigh, you're like piano keys
Ryleigh, you're like ivory
You're gorgeous enough for display,
and more gorgeous to interact, to play
To get you smiling is to make the sun shine twice as bright, but brighter
You captivate me and leave me breathless
Ryleigh, you unleash another side of me, oh Ryleigh, you're like ivory.

Is It Luck?

There's this girl
And this girl
She makes my mind whirl
To the point where I want to twirl
And when you twirl
You're head spins
My head spins for this girl
The feelings I have for her are rural
I've hit uncharted land
Uncharted feelings
And uncharted sand
My love can be compared to a beach
It's long and predictable
But some things about it are unthinkable
My love for you just feels aboriginal and unequivocal
Because I've never felt so much for one person and to me
You are just irresistible
You make me feel something I've never felt before
Something unoriginal
I can try to lie and say I was lucky enough to feel this
But I never have felt this until you
My feelings are just inexplicable
But that must be what this is
Luck
What else can it be?
It must be luck for me to be this lovestruck
Is it luck?

Well, in all actuality, I'm happy
Whether it was just luck or me
I'm just happy it came to be
Being with you
I've never felt so free

Joke

What do you expect me to do?
When I'm living life, and I'm through
I can't handle anymore
Life's a fucking bore
and when I finally get some excitement
It's gone and no more
It came just to leave me
It came just to cease me
I don't know what anyone can ever see in me
Almost everyone in this world wants to be free from me

Life's a joke

Light Gives Sight

The girl you love kissed another man
You walked in as she went to grasp his hand
The sun and window beautiful exposing
Your feelings are broken but opposing

Locked Away

Don't you love when you get compliments?
When someone calls you pretty, maybe gorgeous, attractive...sexy even
What about being told you're made for bondage?
That you have wide hips and a nice neck to wrap their hands around
Have you ever been complimented on how sweet you cry in agony?
Or how beautifully you suffer?

I grew up with my mother,
She neglected me
and I was nothing but not a son to her
My mother. . .
Was just like every other of her kind
No, she would not buy me gifts
Nor jewelry, nor would she buy makeup
Or ever think about it for that matter,
Her money had a different purpose...
Drugs.
She would spend every last cent, if even it meant
We wouldn't have enough to pay rent
And I would cry every last tear because I wished not to be here...
and I'd lament...
Even if it meant that I would gain a slap to the face for being a
disgrace
Even though my mother, Grace, was always lost and didn't know
her place

Yes, she was lost, her parents didn't want her
Maybe she had no sympathy
She was treated so badly, but maybe she deserved it
She would talk about how she worked for everything she had
But she didn't have much

Maybe she had no sympathy, because even though being through the same,
She quickly rid of me
And for what? Something called heroin? To sit still, yet spin?
I suppose my everlasting pain and suffering to her was money in her pocket and something she no longer had to endure
Maybe she was cursed with a sickness, perhaps I was the cause,
Nonetheless, she assumed my agony and absence was the cure,

Where she is in life? I'm not sure
But I wonder almost all the time
Because no person I'm with now, no none, can I have a relationship as pure
It was hell, yes
But I would escape to it in a ring of a bell
At the snap of a finger,
At the snap of a wrist,
And yes, I know very well the sound that such a thing would make,
Oh the first time I shivered and watched another girl shake
With a demon above her
Who shoved her
Who started with saying he loved her,
A demon inside a man
Whose greed and lust captured his image perfectly

He was a worthless creep

I now cope with this,
Because that's my daily life
Men who have a wife, but still desire others, especially those that
do the opposite of admire in their presence.
With each passing day, the surprise lessens
Because these men, they beat it into us
They say they'll teach us some "lessons"
And so we listen because we've already been so abused that we
can't take anything more physical
So we let them feed their greed, and we wind up broken or dead
and still carry their evil seed

One thing that can build light in such a time
If even from such an evil thing
Is a prosperous life, a human being?
But no, we go through the pain of giving,
And we don't get a prosperous life,
Because like I said
My relationship here... will never be as pure...
as it was...when I was with Grace.
So these men
They take our creations
They use them against us
If we slipped up or messed up
Or did the slightest thing they didn't like,
They would bleed, and be beat until they just ripped off their feet
Then, those monsters, would destroy a baby that they saw as a toy
of influence

But yet they don't need such an idea,
This is their world
And they are the ruthless rulers, raging rampant
In this dark, dark, brutal, destructive encampment

I continue my routine
Awaiting my next tear for when I break
but until then, I shiver, and I shake

Never Me

She will never trust you

You're not good enough

But I hope

But that hope ends up hanging by a rope

And I choke

Can't control the feelings she has awoke

My heart always ends up broke

So much pain almost feels like I'm having a stroke

I need soap

I need to wash her out of my mind

No one like her

I'll be able to find

She leaves me hopelessly and emotionally blind

I just want her by my side

Just want her sitting next to me

On a long car ride

Minimally wide

That way she can be closer to my side

But she'll never choose me

I'm not good enough

It will never be me

There will always be...

Someone else

They're together

And I have to see

If he's better

And it will never be me

I'll never be the one to hold her in my arms in front of everyone
I want her to love me like him
But to her, he is at the tip top
Top of the rim
I'm at the base
In a basket, I'm the waste
To her...I'm probably one big disgrace
I try to keep my love at bay
Try to keep a steady pace
She'll never open up
I'll never be able to step up
I never want to give up
But I'll never be first place
At home...my feelings erupt
Without her
I feel so corrupt
I'm not good enough
I don't meet her standards
She thinks so low of you
Something bad happens
She immediately assumes the worst of you
She'll never listen
She'll never trust me
I love her...
Somehow to her...I doubt it feels the same
This isn't a game
At this point
I'm starting to feel real lame
Into my life she came
Nothing ever remained quite the same
I wanted her
I wanted with her what she already had

A flame
I'll never have that
Not with her
Not when she had him
He'll always be better
And what do I do?
I upset her
It will never be me
She'll never trust me
It will never be me
I have to open my eyes
I'm not good enough
If even she says so,
It doesn't feel like it
It feels like it's one big bluff
I'm not good enough
But with her...I can't have enough
Why does life have to be so rough?
I want her
But she'll never want me the same
It's just a game
A game where I do not reign
I lose
I lost
It's not me
I just want to be lost with her
But obviously
From what I can see
She doesn't want the same with me

Love

Love is this interesting thing that can't be defined
Love is this interesting thing that we all try to define
But what is the point of trying to put words to something that you can't put words to
When you say and mean I love you
It's great to hear "I love you, too"
But what if it's not meant to be?
What if those feelings were taken and beat?
What if you're conflicted and can't get in your mind which one would be better
Which one will give to you more?
Which one will be more gifted?
Which one will work?
How long will it last?
What about the past?
It keeps coming up
You keep thinking about it
Did you make the right choice?
Love is weird
It can't be defined
Love is something that can always get intertwined
Sometimes you just have to fight through it
But what if it's not possible or you can't do it?
What if you're on the wrong side of things
Wanting something that's not worth wanting because you can't have it
But as good as love is

It's also bad

Because no matter how much you know you can't get her or him

It doesn't stop you from wanting him or her

Love can put you in awful situations

Situations you never thought would occur

But you would do anything to be with her

Anything to be with him

Maybe if timing were better

They'd want the same

Maybe it just can't work out

But I try anyway just in hopes that something might sprout

Things just can't always go your way

Sometimes love is to blame

Love can put you to shame

Love can also bring you up

But it can put you down

With that comes a frown

But can also come a smile

Even if sometimes you frown

When you smile

It makes you think it was all worth while

But was it?

That depends

Some people hate love just because it ends

They have this beautiful picture in their mind where their love is
endless

But endless doesn't exist

So they throw away everything because they lost love

And love to them IS everything

They get so caught up in love that they consume it

And when they lose it?

They literally lose it

They hate love because theirs couldn't last

But because it didn't last doesn't mean you need to keep getting caught up in your past

You had it

That's one more than a lot of people

But you hate love because despite that you had it

You no longer have it

But forget about all the bad feelings

Don't focus on them

Hate and Love

Those are opposites

They naturally attract but with some hard work

You can fight back all the feelings and the hurt

Just don't let the hate overwhelm you, but if it does

Break through

If you keep finding yourself looking into the past onto something that didn't even last

Just look at the good and know that you had it

Know that you HAD even though you no longer do

But you still want something you can't have

So your heart is starting to split in halves

They mean so much to you

You have already grown attached

And those kinds of feelings you just can't undo

And because of the situation the best you can do is subdue

All I want to do is let loose

But you have to be strong because the feeling of love can also overwhelm you

Love seems endless

That's because when you see them and you get lost in them

All you can think about is them

Time stops

So do you
You think about everything possible you two can do
Things that might be in the future just waiting
The time seemingly stops, and that makes it feel longer
And when that happens it makes you feel a little stronger for her
A little weaker and longing for her
But you have to be stronger for her
Because no matter how much those feelings get stronger or how
much you long for her
Things just aren't right
So you end up leaving her despite

Love Triangle

I'm in a love triangle

and there's only two sides

At the vertex, there is a girl

She has beautiful eyes

And she's caught up between two guys

Eventually, one choice will have to arise

Because I don't want to be just one of two guys

I'm pretty sure she's made her choice

I'm not happy with it

But there's nothing I can do

It's her life

I'll have to move on

But I feel like I have the flu

I'm crying

I feel like I'm close to dying

When I say all there is you

And I love you

I wasn't lying

But now I'm crying

When I say I love you

I couldn't say anything more true

But the love wasn't equal

My true feelings made their debut

But now they will have to dry up

Because all they were was residue

I was following a lost cause

I should've done something the first pause

But I wanted to hope

She said she loved me, too

But there's nothing I can do

Love is just collecting its internal revenue

I tried to see things through

But the waiting is far overdue

She was too good for me

It was too good to be true

I'm glad I at least got to journey this journey with you

In the end, I never saw it working out

But loving you was just something too big and new

So are we done?

Apparently so

You made your decision and told me I need to go

I wanted you to choose me

But that was a far-fetched fantasy

We tried to be friends

That didn't work out

We both seemed to want more

And now I'm more in love with you than ever before

All it does is hurt me and hurt you

We tried to be friends

But all good things come to their ends

Maybe we can be friends one day

When all my feelings mend

I never lied

I tried

I tried and you gave me a lot of pride

In the end you didn't choose me
...so I cried
I just wish things could be different
But everything I say to you is insignificant
Thinking I could have you?
How could I be so ignorant?

Melted Hearts and Millions of Dreams

I swear your smile can melt a thousand hearts
And your eyes can hold a million dreams
Dreams of us where we don't drift apart
I had a dream where we had an actual start
We made it somewhere
Everyone was jealous of us
We lived in New York City with three kids- two girls, one boy
Our oldest, when born
Oh she was beautiful
She was as pretty as her mother, I could've sworn
Her mother was beautiful
So much so it was impossible to adorn
But I adored
Both child and loving mother
Your eyes are gateways of ecstasy
Whenever you look away
I want you to turn back
To let me see
And feel that feeling that sets you free
Lifts you out of reality and into the feeling of utopia
Every moment with her was perfect
Lost in her was like being lost in heaven
I can feel myself lighten from the weight gone
My entire heart without worry
And my mind empty besides you upon

The Calm

The thirtieth of July I've already decided
Many days pass by
And we're still left undivided
Many more await
In this sweet thing called love
And it must be fate

It feels like she came from above
Falling down from the sky
Flying sweeter than even a dove
Something that I can't deny
She was so beautiful
It was hard to even pry an eye

Even when we are distant at times
I'm still reminiscent
Still in a state of mind
Where I still love her
She's tender and kind
No amount of words can describe
Because she can't be defined
Thinking of her just gets my mind intertwined

In her you will find
Something even more bright than light
I love her so much despite
We barely ever even fight
There is no place I wouldn't go for her
Or any height
Because she is my might

I've told her before
And I'm going to tell her a lot more
She's the best decision I made
For sure

She's my oxygen, my heart, my brain
Everything I can't live without
No doubt

There's been rough times
And we pulled through it
It's can be hard too
But we can do it

Even though we've both been through some stuff
And believe me
I won't bluff
No matter how much I have of her
I just cant get enough

You just received this gift
It's near your birthday
And our anniversary
Just know I'll accept you
And any diversity
No matter what
I will always stay
And no matter what you say
I love you more
Yours will never be able to outweigh
Never mind, I don't feel like arguing
So I'll cut you some slack
You can say we love each other equally
And I can say it back

prickle sunshine dandelion

flower, find me,
i do not wish to look,
flower, find me,
i need you as my nook,
to go to, soak through,
and be my pretty hook,
to hang on, depend on,
and love with all my heart,
pretty flower, too pretty to pluck,
pretty flower, take all my luck,
sunshine watches,
and washes over us,
let us unite, blessed by a buzz,
bee mine once again,
let me feel the sting,
bee flight, bee fly, right over me,
take me with you,
i want to see the sky,
into heavens, but i do not wish to die,
take me with you, and pollinate my soul,
pretty flower, please be at ease,
let's release... our power,
and soak in the morning shower,
one day with you, would suffice,
but my heart follows, even into demise,
i see you, flower, let me look into your eyes,
pretty petals, what a beautiful face,
see me, please me, please be in my arms

See Ya Later

The feelings I have are so massive
that it's hard to be able to say they are there
Their hold on me is so powerful that it is hard to realize it hasn't
always been,
It cradles over me and to it I am numb

My heart shall ache and pain me for many thoughts and time to come
The feeling of moving away from everything you have known
and severing the close bond that has always been one
It is a feeling of disaster, of ripping.
It saddens me, and for now I am numb

It shall come out in waves until it is finally done
We are not saying goodbye, and we shall reunite as one

Realization

In reply to your poem
I always wanted to see one of them
But you would never show 'em
I never wanted a poem for my own
I just wanted to see your poems
Have you open up to me
Show me what it's like to be you
Inside your mind
The place that I always found to be one of the sweetest of its kind
You rarely opened up to me
But when you did, knowingly, you didn't want pity
But some things in life are real shitty

I can guarantee that with you I never felt so free
That is
When you didn't confine me
When you might actually confide in me
Didn't make me stray away
When you didn't break me
And make my heart fly astray

I never lied to you
I always told the truth
It's not my fault you didn't believe in me
It's all the others that broke you
You are dreaming
I just wanted to see you awoke

I wanted to be able to one day. . .roll over and awake. . .next to you
My fingers in your hair. . .to stroke
One day, I hoped to share a moment under the crescent just laying
on your breast
Just for a second, a moment that would be fluorescent

She was gone for the moments that you were still true for me
Remember the simple times when you just let loose with me?
I'm still blue
With me, you were through
I just wanted you
I wanted you to kiss me
I wanted you to tell me that you missed me and just have kissed me
That maybe you wished for me...

You set flame your biggest fears that never before had to be feared
If you just believed in me...
But my heart was left seared from those flames that made me get
speared
and left feeling like game
Who is to blame?
I can tell you, if the blame is on me, it is not just me
If you can look at things from my perspective, just see
Your fears were nothing but imagination
But you made them more and set me into desperation
Desperation for your love that you discontinued

Not better
She just didn't keep me waiting
On the edge
Just waiting
Feeling everything locked inside

With no one to confide
Locked away inside
Every day, I cried
Long nights of restlessness
Ignored and desperate since
Desperate for your forgiveness that you never gave
Forgiveness that shouldn't even exist because the issue was not real
Our relationship
Fake issues consistent
You were enough
Even more so
More than enough
I'd give up everything for you
But this stuff, you brought upon yourself
Even if you didn't mean to or realize it
You were enough but you did this to yourself

You should have believed me
I never spoke a word that wasn't true
You say you trusted me
You rarely did
You never believed me
You say you did
If you trusted me and believed me
Things wouldn't be the way they are
You didn't put everything into me
If you did...you would've kissed me

If I ever meant anything to you
You wouldn't dispose me
Maybe compose of me...
But not dispose of me

You would've chosen me?
Well you didn't
You left me waiting
Constantly contemplating
And stating how you are an underrating
But you never rung it in
You never made it so
I was contemplating your love for me
If it ever would've gone my way
You should've kissed me
I told you I needed it
That was my way of seeing if we would make it
Even if you just faked it...

Those feelings that you got from my hand, they were shared
Mutual ecstatic feelings that ran through my body, soul, to every end
That feeling too, drove me insane
But it put me in pain that you wouldn't even look at me
Didn't seem that you had faith in me
For that I had no strength
I needed you to tell me you need me
Just share eye contact with me
Believe in me
Know I wouldn't hurt you
And it would be so
If being turned to "dust" puts me in pain
For that feeling that once drove me insane
Still does
It lingers in my hands
My nerves
Longing for maybe another one
Another day with you...under the sun

Why attempt to forget something that made you so happy?
Forcing something out of your mind isn't exempting
At times, it might seem tempting
But you'll forget and not learn
Learn what it feels like for someone to truly love you
With everything they have, with no reason to ever want to bring hurt
To me, you were the biggest prize of them all, of any in the world
If you just stopped messing with my emotions and just set in motion us
I was ready to spend an entire lifetime with you
To do everything it took, until the moment we say "I do"

I realize I was perfect
The issue was you
And you were perfect
You had no flaw besides not trusting me
Believing me, assuming the worst of me
But I never lied, and I was perfect,
Especially considering the circumstances
You made me do emotional dances
If love was a game,
You played your game wrong

Seek This

I resent your heart
For ripping me apart
For shredding me to pieces
And bringing out weakness

Sidewalk Thoughts

I hope you know it took all the will power in the world to not
shed a tear
All the will power in the world not to set sight on my fear
I'm walking on the sidewalk
Remembering our old talks
Going home without realizing it
Because home isn't what it used to be
Playing the game of life
There has always been a set fee
Making it to the end is when you'll finally be set free
Alone in a world of simulation
Driven by your mind, the center of creation
A world full of imitation
Feeling a need for a destination in this simulation of creation
A world that never used to be filled with limitation

Sit Out

I hate everything
I thought I was set
I thought everything was going to be well
Every single thing will be swell
It will all come together, it will gel

No, it turned into a living hell
Constant ringing, church bells
Time is the only thing that can tell
Keep in mind your instincts
They can smell- that shit stinks
They can tell when things are distinct

It's sweeping...
The pain is.
Weeping... my eyes are
Locking... heart in jar

Electric feelings were electric, deadly shock
No more feelings in stock
You're out of luck
We're all sold out
I know with that price you were struck
I had doubt, but nevertheless there will be others about

Knowing this, I still internally hurt and shout
I'm not the same without
Now I await the oncoming emotional drought
Love? I think I'll sit this one out

Serenade Me

Sing me a song,
So I can sing along,
Sing me something sweet
That will lift me from my feet,

Life is dramatic, and I need to hear you sing,
Life is chaotic, and I need to feel your sting.

Step and Unroll; Step all over my Heart

it's crazy how love can so betray

when you lay your heart out like a carpet

and keep it open while they still stay

and step all over it when it runs astray,

and wants to be curled up and put away

go on as you will atop another hill,

step on more carpets along your way,

none will be tall enough to hold you up as you wish,

reaching your ego, even for you, will only ever be fantasy,

you dirty them with your shoes,

you cuddle them until they rip loose,

you sink into them, as they sponge your insanity and ego,

you make them so dependent they don't want to let go

so precious, kind, and forgiving they were,

as you stepped on them, and they saw you as pure,

that you did not mean to hurt,

but only never knowing would be the cure, so that's what they think,

yet how can they even hold in their heart the knowledge of what
they do,

without convincing themselves their intentions were honest and true,

to justify any actions with fakeness and lies,

running away from yourself, always in disguise,

only such evil masked by fake purity in your eyes,

only fantasy holds you as an angel,

and love creates fantasy,

and the heart creates a carpet to be opened and abused

Induce the Agony

They talked all night
Jack with no strength, no might
Lost the battle
Lost the fight
The decision was made
He would fade
But she won't
She was his world
And without her, he felt life was impossible
He didn't want to live without her
But her choice was getting clear
He was already upset, filled with fear
More crying and more tears
He realized again how his chances were slim
So he knew how hard it was for him
Jack let out his rage, let out his anger
To get him away from her
He couldn't do it himself
She needed to do it
So he was upset and filled with dispute, and harsh words he threw
His blood boiling up and him burning inside like a stew
Left aside, painful to coincide
The pain
World dripping with rain
Life isn't so great
It's pain
Without her

It will NEVER be the same
But to her, he doesn't blame
He doesn't even have any shame
He loved every second
Up until the end
He lost a great person and a great friend
And gained a wound that would never mend
Lightheaded from the crying
Put a knife to his wrist, nothing happened
He wanted it easy
He wanted an out
Suffocation didn't work, his instincts kicked in
Slammed his head into a wall
Paint scatters and a mirror falls
Ran to the nearest shoe
Took the shoelace out
His life is filled with doubt
He tied it tight around his neck
Breathing by the minute was getting harder
He was getting scared
He wanted it easy
He was getting lightheaded and queasy
Jack picked up the knife he carried with him
He tried to cut it off
But it was so tight, it would get him, too
He didn't want blood, that he couldn't do
He burned it off and it hurt really bad
Still filled with sad
Pills on the counter, what a beautiful encounter
Some unopened, others not
He swallowed many pills
This is it

I won
Runs out the door
Slams it
Fallen to his knees
Cold air, cold breeze
Nauseous and loss of balance
Stomping
Loud stomping
Caught
Why are all the pills gone?
What have you done?
I can't leave you unsupervised, can I?
Did you swallow them?
Get inside, gag them out
He stuck his fingers down his throat, no success
The place was torn apart, it was a mess
He gave him something that made him puke it up
Jack was sent to bed
Next day to find out they started dating yesterday
Yesterday. . .